FRANNY CHOI

The World K
and the Wo

The World Keeps Ending, and the World Goes On

Franny Choi

An Imprint of HarperCollins*Publishers*

HarperCollins books may be purchased for educational, business, or sales promotional use. For information, please email the Special Markets Department at SPsales@harpercollins.com.

Ecco® and HarperCollins® are trademarks of HarperCollins Publishers.

FIRST EDITION

Designed by Angela Boutin
Title page and part opener images © Irina/stock.adobe.com

Library of Congress Cataloging-in-Publication Data has been applied for.

ISBN 978-0-06-324008-7

23 24 25 26 27 LBC 8 7 6 5 4

For my parents and grandparents

CONTENTS

II

III

IV

V

**The World Keeps Ending,
and the World Goes On**

THE WORLD KEEPS ENDING, AND THE WORLD GOES ON

Before the apocalypse, there was the apocalypse of boats:

boats of prisoners, boats cracking under sky-iron, boats making corpses

bloom like algae on the shore. Before the apocalypse, there was the apocalypse

of the bombed mosque. There was the apocalypse of the taxi driver warped

by flame. There was the apocalypse of the leaving, and the having left—

of my mother unsticking herself from her mother's grave

as the plane barreled down the runway. Before

the apocalypse, there was the apocalypse of planes.

There was the apocalypse of pipelines legislating their way through sacred water,

and the apocalypse of the dogs. Before which was the apocalypse of the dogs

and the hoses. Before which, the apocalypse of dogs and slave catchers

whose faces glowed by lantern light. Before the apocalypse,

the apocalypse of bees. The apocalypse of buses. Border fence

apocalypse. Coat hanger apocalypse. Apocalypse in the textbook's

selective silences. There was the apocalypse of the settlement

and the soda machine; the apocalypse of the settlement and

the jars of scalps; there was *the bedlam of the cannery*; the radioactive rain;

the chairless martyr demanding a name. I was born from an apocalypse

and have come to tell you what I know—which is that the apocalypse began

when Columbus praised God and lowered his anchor. It began when a continent was drawn into cutlets. It began when Kublai Khan told Marco, *Begin*

at the beginning. By the time the apocalypse began, the world had already ended.

It ended every day for a century or two. It ended, and another ending

world spun in its place. It ended, and we woke up and ordered Greek coffees,

drew the hot liquid through our teeth, as everywhere, the apocalypse rumbled,

the apocalypse remembered, our dear, beloved apocalypse—it drifted

slowly from the trees all around us, so loud we finally stopped hearing it.

I

Where did the way lead when it led nowhere?

—*Paul Celan*

CATASTROPHE IS NEXT TO GODLINESS

Lord, I confess I want the clarity of catastrophe but not the catastrophe.

Like everyone else, I want a storm I can dance in.

I want an excuse to change my life.

The day A died, the sun was brighter than any sun.

I answered the phone, and a channel opened

between my stupid head and heaven, or what was left of it. The blankness

stared back; and I made sound after sound with my blood-wet gullet.

O unsayable—O tender and divine unsayable, I knew you then:

you line straight to the planet's calamitous core; you moment moment moment;

you intimate abyss I called sister for a good reason.

When the Bad Thing happened, I saw every blade.

And every year I find out what they've done to us, I shed another skin.

I get closer to open air, true north. Lord,

if I say, *Bless the cold water you throw on my face,*

does that make me a costume party. Am I greedy for comfort

if I ask you not to kill my friends—if I beg you to press your heel

against my throat—please, not enough to ruin me,

but just so—just so I can almost see your face—

DISASTER MEANS "WITHOUT A STAR"

Sixty-six million years after the end of the world, I click *purchase*

on an emergency go-bag from Amazon. When it arrives, I'll use my teeth

to tear open the plastic, unzip the pack stitched by girls who look like me

but for their N95s, half a judgment day away, no evacuation plan in sight.

Another episode of the present tense, and I can't stop thinking

about the time line where the asteroid misses, Earth ruled eternally

by the car-hearted and walnut-brained. Meanwhile, I'm merely gorging

on the butterfly effects of ashes, ashes; reaching for the oat milk

while, hundreds of feet below, a chalk line marks the moment we were all

doomed. We were done for. We were science fiction before science,

or fiction. One billion judgment days later, I'm alive and ashamed

of my purchases; I'm afraid of being afraid; I'm the world's worst mother.

My sister calls, and it's already too late for things to be better. Every mistake,

an asteroid that's already hit, history already mushroomed into one million species

of unfit, their fossilized corpses already forming coastlines, austere offices.

This year was a layer cake of catastrophe long before any of us could,

biologically speaking, have been imagined. Human History, a front parlor
infinitely painted over with massacre, and into the fray came I, highly allergic,
quick to cry, and armed with fat fists of need. I broke everything I touched.
I got good grades. I was told nothing was more noble than to ensure

my children would eat. I learned to take a chicken apart with my hands,
to fill in a Scantron, cry on cue. Sixty-six million years after the last
great extinction, six to eight business days before the next one, I whispered
Speak to a fucking agent into the hold music to trigger the system into connecting

me with a "real person." I avoided coughing in public, though it was too late.
I applied for a BIPOC farming intensive, though it was too late for the earth
to yield anything but more corpses. New species of horror sequence
were already evolving: election bot; cluster bio-bomb; driverless wife.

I muttered curses to keep the deep fakes away, studied the stars for signs
of the worlds to come, though they were already here—the extinctions
and feudal lords, the dirty blankets, the dissidents tied to stakes or hung
from branches, the price gouge, death camp, flood, bombs of liberty, bomb

and bomb and bomb already dropped, already having made me

from its dust, already broken and paid for and straddling my crown.

What crown? If I'm king of anything, it's being late. *Omw*, I type,

though I'm still huddled in last year's mistakes. *Asteroid*, Alexa corrects,

and I say, *Five minutes. Just give me five minutes. I'll be right there.*

POEM WITH AN END IN SIGHT

I don't have a brain for anything

that's happening on-screen. I don't

have a brain for the men yelling over

each other, *I've done an amazing job,*

their cheeks flushed and flaking. I've done

an amazing job. I have two degrees

and couldn't have saved anyone, *couldn't*

have saved a dog. I have a million ideas.

I have last year's ashes in my throat, stories

stuffed so full of morals they bleed sugar.

Midnight, and my stomachs drag

like nets through a river. Dawn,

and I'm out on the blacktop, praying

to no one, so no one prays back.

I know I should want to be torn open

by the failures of hope, but here's what I want:

a tight circle around everyone I love;

a stove that doesn't burn. O year,

O shitstorm, it's impossible to be alive, impossible

to be dead. So, brainlessly, I tongue the news

again, instead. I have no condition but this:

ill-timed optimism; a disturbing tendency

toward pleasure; also, bad at reading tone.

For example, is this a hopeful poem,

or a hopeless one? If I write, *there's nothing*

to be done, it's a bird in the hand, i.e.,

worth its weight in dead bird. It's so corny

to call for the tyrant's head again, and yet.

CELEBRATE GOOD TIMES

The regime is having a birthday party, so we turn off the lights

    and pretend we're sick. All night, happy Americans

honk their horns. *We did it*, they scream into our window.

    In the morning, *We* is all over the floor. We sweep *We*

into a paper bag and label it *EMERGENCY.* The good news

    is that things will go back to the way they were,

which is also the bad news. Meanwhile, I cut

    an onion, and it's onions all the way down, and that's a fine

reason to cry at the sink on a Monday after the empire

    congratulates itself on persisting again. No, thank you,

I'm stuffed, I couldn't possibly have more hope. I haven't finished

    mourning the last tyrant yet. I haven't said enough

goodbyes to—oh, what was her name? And hers?

How many *We*s did they cut out of me? And whose country

was I standing on, the last time we survived?

GOOD MORNING AMERICA

Headline: the unthinkable's already, already

happened again—and so Layleen's perfect face

swings back into the orbit of my grief—

Catch up—it's the anniversary of the aftermath

of another bad massacre, and I've got

plenty of seats. *Come in*, I whisper

to the wailing in the attic, *Come in* to the thunder,

to any sound that'll shake me from doom's haze.

Dispatches from Kenosha,

Louisville, Atlanta, arrive, arrive

like a steady kickdrum of sparrows

spatchcocked by gravity, little nevers,

little couldn'ts; too late to stop the video,

too late, too late. I hold each stolen face

against my forehead as the centuries slough off,

flightless. Century and its scythes. Century

and its literal marks and mobs. As a child,

I couldn't believe my luck: born

in the best country on Earth.

Now I know better. So what.

Good morning, what's done is done is.

Come in, last year's wreck, rent.

Grief's a heavy planet, and green.

I know better than to call

each gravity's daughter to my softest cheek.

I know, and I know.

So what?

IT IS WHAT IT IS

Each morning, on her way

to make a living, my mother passes

that business, now closed, where—

I've tried not to think of it—

a man killed three Korean mothers

just like mine.

Her voice echoes, heavy,

into the tunnel between us:

What am I supposed to do?

Be afraid?

What am I supposed to do?

In the tunnel between us,

her voice echoes, heavy

just like mine.

A man killed three Korean mothers.

I've tried not to think of it.

That business, now closed. Where

to make a life? My mother passes

each morning on her way.

SCIENCE FICTION POETRY

Dystopia of the lost file;

Dystopia of the cracked screen;

Dystopia of the ankle prone to getting sprained again;

Dystopia of house plants gone yellow and headless;

Dystopia between people who have hurt each other too many times to
keep speaking;

Dystopia too sad to shower;

Dystopia a cake made of water;

Dystopia of back in prison but at least they'll get clean;

Dystopia of living in your last body;

Dystopia all day in an air-conditioned conference hall with no sweater;

Dystopia of falling out of love with God;

Dystopia of houseless people and boarded-up houses on the same city block;

Dystopia of solitary confinement as an answer to any any;

Dystopia of cages; dystopia of forgetting about cages;

Dystopia bail out the coal plants if you want to live;

Dystopia of billionaires racing giddy to space;

Dystopia $800 a month but the debt stays the same;

Dystopia very lonely on Mother's Day;

Dystopia very small in rooms;

Dystopia bone-tired after hours at home;

Dystopia can't read a book without thinking about the trees;

Dystopia can't talk about it without panicking;

Dystopia of hold music;

Dystopia of platitudes;

Dystopia of garbled logic spun and spun in the head;

Dystopia congratulations you were right to be paranoid;

Dystopia of diversity trainings;

Dystopia of the banning of diversity trainings;

Dystopia of the disobedient muscle; the inflexible algorithm;

Dystopia of the algorithm's smooth skin and dulcet reasoning;

Dystopia of poorly designed public restrooms; dystopia of restrooms;

Dystopia I liked the old dystopia better;

Dystopia paying money for water;

Dystopia $2.13 an hour before tips; meanwhile billionaires in space;

Dystopia sixty hours a week in a pandemic;

Dystopia fill out this form if you get raped;

Dystopia in ankle bracelets, and in coworkers joking *house arrest*;

Dystopia of the city council hearing *Thank you for your comment*;

Dystopia in the Senate hearing *Not to my knowledge I was not aware*;

Dystopia on loop over the airport speakers; on loop in the fine print;

Dystopia *I have read the terms and conditions*;

Dystopia everything I eat is touched with money; dystopia everything I am
  is touched;

Dystopia press your thumb here to access your memories;

Dystopia to stop remembering one's memories;

Dystopia to keep remembering one's memories;

Dystopia to be flattened or flared at a memory's notice; at a hair;

otherwise, to drift

numb and dreaming through the so-called day;

Dystopia isn't there something else besides; there must be;

some sequence that ends in anything but a cold loop; there must be

an elsewhere on the else side of the scrim; an opposite word

but not that one; please;

not sticky with sap; not synthetic sugar and cruel;

what's the other opposite

world; if we knew its name

could we call it; if we called it would it come;

WE USED OUR WORDS WE USED WHAT WORDS WE HAD

we used our words we used what words we had

to weld, what words we had we wielded, kneeled,

we knelt. & wept we wrung the wet the sweat

we racked our lips we rang for words to ward

off sleep to warn to want ourselves. to want

the earth we mouthed it wound our vowels until

it fit, in fits the earth we mounted roused

& rocked we harped we yawned & tried to yawp

& tried to fix, affixed, we facted, felt.

we fattened fanfared anthemed hammered, felt

the words' worth stagnate, snap in half in heat

the wane the melt what words we'd hoarded halved

& holey, porous. meanwhile tide still tide.

& we: still washed for sounds to mark. & marked.

DANEZ SAYS THEY WANT TO LOSE THEMSELVES IN BOPS THEY CAN'T SING ALONG TO

and I'm thinking of the years I spent sweating

to the choreo of every K-pop song with a decent

dance break, me and the other girls from church,

practically saintly in our diligence as we

rehearsed our isolations and body rolls, re-

and rewinding the tapes, our noses nearly

grazing the screen, though in truth I only understood

maybe about half the words, the other half

mostly sounds which nevertheless sank

into my muscles, pathways laid by so many

hours of industrious mouthing that now,

while humming idly some stupid tune

at the sink, I'll realize for the first time ever

what! that line meant (though of course

pop everywhere's a language so reliable

it's nearly nothing, *baby let me know* and

I need you in my arms on babbling loop

through the ages), and I'm thinking, too,

about how this, my first love of losing myself in

the scaffolds and percussives of an unparsed lyric

doomed me for life to never be able to hear,

actually hear, the words to any songs, even

in English, even my favorites, like Jamila's,

which I put on when I'm adrift and sunken and just need

to feel at home in something—even those

harbors are built, mostly, of sonics—

not gibberish, I mean, but language so sacred

it's not my place to try to decipher it,

phonemes holy as stones on a string, mysterious

as the names we give to animals, or words

we know only in prayer—at Rebecca's mother's funeral,

for example, where, when invited, I added my small voice

to the reciting of the Kaddish, and the perfect

thunder of it lifted one part of me higher

than air, while rooting another

deep into the fragrant earth, a bit of which

I later scooped, as gently as I could bear,

onto the casket, the shovel heavier than any

word I knew, and more full of light

than even the birds overhead, who,

as we wept, kept, of course, right on saying

exactly whatever they needed to say.

I HAVE BAD NEWS AND BAD NEWS, WHICH DO YOU WANT FIRST

with thanks to Brigit Pegeen Kelly

One week ago, my mother had two COVID patients.

Now, she has thirty. *What?* I say. *When did that happen?*

though *when*'s not the question I mean. The video's—

> *Try not to time travel*, says the voice in my meditation app,
>
> as I fast-forward to everything I haven't yet remembered
>
> to be afraid of—

got a lag, so my mother's words float somewhere slightly

to the right of her mouth, chronologically. Somewhere

in the ventriloquized future, she is already delivering—

> I keep dreaming about showing up late to my own funeral,
>
> everyone tapping their feet as I climb into the casket—

the news. I've told everyone I know, *I'm worried*

about my mother, not realizing it's not true until I hear her voice.

And then, suddenly, it is, and I drop into the fear like—

I don't yet have a memory of my mother's death,

only the time S and I talked about being afraid; even then

we couldn't look at anything but the bloom-strung sky—

a pool, like the lights of a bad holiday hammering down

my arms in loud droplets—bright globules like that, like actual skin—

like that—I try to stretch the feeling into a syntax—*like*—

like to bully a feeling into the thought of a feeling—

like preparing for ruin by running the fear of it dry—no—

like a *hand*—   pressing my *hand* into my *incredibly lifelike heart*—

pinning myself into *the pool's floor*—no.

pinning myself into myself—yes. Draping the weight

of the breath of it, the moment of it—yes—into my *scatterbrained*

clock:

no. Into my chest, my only chest—I swear—

When did it happen:

my whole life rotted into predicting my last

life's last moments—the great metal tolling as everyone I love drains
back-
wards out of our coils into the great scream of space, will it happen—
when will it happen—

I'm okay, say the ventriloquized pixels of my mother.
I don't believe her.

I've skipped too far ahead. A few dozen years, and it won't be true.

A hundred, and I'll never know I knew.

GRIEF IS A THING WITH TENSE ISSUES

In the grocery store, I gently squeeze every avocado. When people stare, I say, "Don't criticize my mourning process!" When they smile reassuringly, it just makes things worse. So I walk out, reciting:

"Denial, anger, bargaining. Denied, angered, bargained. Will deny, will anger, will bargain."

    . . .

The problem with using a word like "mourning" in reference to the future. As when a mother in a movie says to her gay son, "You're dead to me." She mistakes glow for a grave, but there he is, red constellation of coals.

Here's something I can say about us: we're not dead, not yet. (Not anymore.)

    . . .

Q: What's the point of grieving in the future tense?

A: Let me tell you this now so you know before you don't know anything:

You were good. You lasted. And at last you were—I mean, you *had been*.

You will *had been*.

I *will have missed* your *is*. Do you know that? Will you have / known that?

        : : :

On the phone, I ask my mother about a memory. Am I mourning that right, I want to know. "Just pretend it didn't happen. I just say, it didn't happen," she says. It happened. Am I saying that right?

What happened?

Did it *happened?*

        : : :

everyone / you know / someday / will die

will was / will used to / will had been

what knew / would have / forgotten

were to / have known / were to have been / lived

: : :

I sit on the train toward Chicago and mourn the avocado softening in my kitchen. This, too, is practice, avocado being the smallest unit of grief. It's rock and ripe and gone; rock and ripe and gone. Which should be a lesson.

Instead, of course, the fruit is another imagination that passes through me on its way to unknowing.

: : :

Q: Is it possible to experience anticipatory feelings toward the past?

A: A whole, gaping, pulsing as I run toward it, though it's the running that pushes it away. In other words, the event is horizonal; an event horizon mothering itself.

. . .

Q: What is the past tense of "lived"?

A: Once, I looked back and purchased vowel after vowel. I devoured the minutes which had already been dripping from my teeth. I smashed the fruit against the bowl and called it "salvage." I retraced my steps, then retraced the retracing. What could I have done? I'll say it every night before the day slips into rot: What could I have done?

. . .

They'll say: What was it like to have so many people on Earth at once?

They won't say that, but I'll answer anyway:

It was very busy. There was always something to avoid.

: : :

I'm softening around my stone. I'm browning into dearth. Into dirt.

Mother, you taught me a word from *from* and never *toward*.

If you speed on ahead, earth forbid, I'll know. I knew.

I dreamt of you stoneless, once. I know, still.

That it was you. Somehow, I'll knew.

COMFORT POEM

Half crumpled on the couch as another bloody world churns

in my belly, I find myself strangely comforted by the laptop's warmth,

despite what I know about radiation, coltan mining, Apple's

growing surveillance empire, on and on. Still,

the fan purrs in the same key as the cat,

whose attention I'm thrilled finally to have earned—

a bit of living warmth when she rubs her cheek against my chin.

A bit of sweet, and touch; it's hard these days;

you get it. Sometime in the last world,

we drove to R's with some post-top-surgery comfort food:

homemade sundubu, in a big Dutch oven wrapped in three towels

on my lap, and the stew, being sour and spicy and made of stuff

that would keep, shared its heat with my torso like an old friend,

a cheery host, a comfort,

. : :

When, prone on the couch, I read it again

comfort

when I read the phrase   *comfort woman*   again
and say it, again, out loud:

comfort woman

comfort   *woman*

comfort woman

      when I read it

bottle   woman

balm   woman

shhh   woman

         bit of living proof amid the war woman

     it's hard these days but at least there's this woman

         girl body bisected by military cock woman

       crawling into the fields to vomit black woman

       rotten rice and blood rag stuffed deep woman

consort woman   *convert woman*   *condom, reused*

    whatever helps you bear the day

    whatever sweet, what touch

     : : :

how to speak to any one in a history like this.

how to tell you.

everything will be all right.

without inheriting.

the family business.

: : :

you who wants comfort, who are you?

have you been   a *comfort*   too?

say it with me: *it won't be okay*

and we can follow the burning shore.

there's nothing more to say. no next time

but the broken before.

II

This sense of impending catastrophe is an illusion,
however, because the trauma never quite arrives.
It never arrives because it has already happened.

—*Grace M. Cho*

PROCESS NOTE

Depending on when and through which education system you learned about so-called world history, you may understand the 1945 atomic bombings of Hiroshima and Nagasaki to represent two things: one, the end of World War II, and two, the end of the world itself—by which I mean not only the destruction of two full cities with their many thousands of individual worlds within them, but also, perhaps, the end of modernity; the ringing in of a half-century-plus of annihilative paranoia and very confusing novels; in other words, the end of narrative; in other words, the end of God. You might picture the hellish clouds captured in those infamous newsreels, or think of the hundreds of thousands of civilians killed, the generations bearing witness via lesion and limb; you might consider whether the United States would have done this to a blonde country, or consider the way a horror like that might burrow into the stuff of a people, not just its genes, but its jokes, the shapes of its crosswalks, the lines of its art. Now. Depending on whether or not you were raised by the descendants of the survivors of a former colony of the Japanese Empire, you might understand the 1945 atomic bombings of Hiroshima and Nagasaki to, in fact, represent *three* things: one, the end of World War II; two, the end of the world itself; and three, the prelude to liberation—the beginning of the end, that is, of the control, carnage, forced labor, and cultural genocide that raped, enslaved, and killed millions of Koreans, Indonesians, Taiwanese, and others. Depending on when and in which geopolitical context you learned "world history," the moment in which you encounter this third association (at the dinner table with your parents, home for some holiday) might sharpen the room around you into sick bloom, as the terrible line appears—not drawn by anything like righteousness, or grim duty, or God, or even causation, really; just the flat time signature of sequence; terrible, indifferent sequence, which leads from the detonations, to carnage, to freedom(?), to carnage, to an airplane in the sky carrying a woman carrying a clumsy gathering of cells that will one day look backwards and see, in that line, only endings, endings, endings—

Sliced from bone, my life
hung like a jaw—faultless. And
unforgivable.

WHO DIED AND MADE YOU AMERICAN

In the afterlife of apocalypse, my people,
too, are settlers of a theft. *Pay me like a man*
whose ancestors burned down the homes

of Pequot children.　　　　Deserve, deserve,
what a sad little word. I'm an upstanding citizen
of a country far from earned. I'm a child

of immigrants, of strategic importance,
of imports from one immolation
to another. Pay my honest mother

in taxes and guilt. If the land in me could speak
to the land I live on, what would it say?
Maybe *I'm sorry.* Or, *where does it hurt?*

My cheeks are stuffed with sweetgrass
and ssuk. Maybe I'm only ever singing
that awful song: *O beautiful.*

O beautiful. And it is, some days,
driving through the "untouched" hills
to the place where I'm paid.

POEM IN PLACE OF A POEM

우리 *family* 를 생각해,

says my mother, as she begs me

not to print my earliest memory

of the police. (I've written it

elsewhere: the cold night.

The parking lot. The cop's jaw

stomping out my mother's pleas.

The vulgar clink of cuffs.

In the poem, her wail rises

like a monument to nothing.

In the memory, no grammar

I can wave at the cop

is enough to keep her safe.)

I need the story, I say, *to explain.*

Why I'm writing about this.

She ends the call crying.

The sound, a hole

where a word might go. Here,

too, I've failed to protect her

from my need. From the cops.

From *mother* and the seeds

of shame. Shame. I've failed again

and again, in any tongue,

to free us.

REMEMORY

Atlanta / Seoul / Kwangju

Whose story was I remembering when riot cops closed in

on all four sides, and a sound happened from somehow me?

The sound was a sound from 1980—year my father was a young man.

Year of bayonets; year of soldiers shooting into crowds, limbs on fire.

My father was a student of biology in another year of martial law,

in a century of war. Bayonet of interruption—my father touched diagrams,

threw rocks at riot gear and wondered what for. It was another year

when they shut the school gates, and students died in the street.

The crowds were gassed and ran choking from the scene.

This year, someone else's father is a young man, choking, and the crowds

are gassed, and we run, boots on the ground. I remember:

this night, this year; no route out of the cops' kettle; me in the crowd, shouting Americanly until the cops study forward with their shields

and fists and then, someone unremembered inside me is wailing; wailing;

someone else's song crawling backwards from my mouth. Whose song:

Hell of looking. Bodies in a heap. Mother-shrieks in white hemp.

Boots on the ground—boots? on the bloody ground? Whose voice was that.

Whose year is it. *Whose streets.* This city, this *our*—slow bayonet of claiming,

whose tank in my mouth? Bayonet of this: American me, fathering nothing

but the wails of strangers I'll never caress. Bayonet of dispersal, gas.

We run, choking on the sound of century and century's return.

I run, and a country breaks its way out of me, then breaks, breaks.

AMID RISING TENSIONS ON THE KOREAN PENINSULA

Your country's memory is short. But know this:

We live, have been living, with this threat

staining the earth we still call home

to mark what happened. The choices

made in the dry mouths of children,

sewn straight into our breasts. We live—

have to live somewhere. Why not

smother doubt to save the family

we're responsible for. The only sunlight

is this story spun from the records,

and we've taken its name as our own. Yes, we

sob and shudder, yes, and feed our babies,

our *our*, our precious claim to *our—*

We can still hear the planes' deathknell hum—

circling our heads like we were carrion,

despite the pictures, which know only how

to tell one truth at a time. Our names were

napalm, ravaged paddies, lung cancer. Names,

like ghosts, reverberate. The bad memories

in the body? They climb to the surface,

from war's muck. War: the only surname

on our unmarked graves. Our sustenance

amidst your savage freeze. So we married fear,

salvaged these small lives. We're free, at least, to

dream of the fires that made us by splitting

the *us* we almost, some days, remember.

DISINHERITANCE

My grandmother fled to avoid being taken.
To avoid being taken, my grandmother wed

early. To avoid being stolen, I stripped
myself of scent. I rubbed in salt till I bled.

Everywhere, the smell of soldiers, and ahead,
kelp—its rot, wafting. My grandmother wed

and ran south with her husband. He was
so much older. He was another kind of soldier.

My grandmother and I were born already lifted out
of the picture. We were born from the smell

of soldiers trying to make an emptiness
where we once stood. Empire, and then, empire

scrubbed our country of its reek—a blessing.
I stand at the beach to watch history unrot,

unwaft, walk back into the water. So long, origin-
storyteller. By the way, my grandmother's mother

was either scraped from the earth during the war, or
she never existed in the first place.

I can't imagine it: her face.
I was born and she was already gone.

I was born, and my grandmother
was already wed and lifted and left

alone with eight children and so much
of the story already nothing. So yes,

I feel most like my grandmother when someone

is scraping my name out of me. I feel most

like my grandmother's mother when I'm already

gone. When I'm peeled down to my seam.

When I lift my skin and smell—nothing. No rot.

No story. Not even the emptiness of salt.

SEPTEMBER 2001

We were punished and salt-licked and wrecked with wanting

we didn't understand. We were old enough to be obsessed

with death—to dream of baseball bats and crushed skulls,

to tongue scripture and lift our wetness toward extinction.

It was the year 2001. And all day, kids got pulled out of class,

so slow and dreamlike it was like they'd dissolved, like the last scene

in *The Sandlot*, boy after boy forever fading into a VHS afterlife.

At lunch, Jackie said, *We finally get our own war,* and everyone knew

it was bad of her to say so, and laughed anyway. I was old enough

to have wanted to run away from home, old enough to be grateful

for my American certificates, to let the prophecies of plague

string my spine with lights. Everything I didn't know was a throatful

of something hot and bothered: the hair crawling up my calves;

the shock that flew through me when Alex drew a picture of sex;

the wreckage of birds I became when he felt me up in the hallway. I didn't

know what to call that feeling, only that I was on the edge of something as impressive and glorious as catastrophe, counting my life mostly

as a series of small, terrible stories: *elsewhere, children are being beaten*

in factories; beaten if they don't speak Japanese; stripped from their bones

if they're born in the wrong country. That year, I fumbled everywhere

for some authorized trajectory through my short-legged life.

Any book could whisper a word to me that would name it,

the exact shiver buzzing at my edges when night lifted

her foreign dress, when Omar's soccer friend called me a chink,

or when the church girls laughed until I was sticky with fire—

you have to understand; it was 2001. We had made it through

the prophesied apocalypse, with its computerized rapture

and bunkers full of pudding. Instead, there had been fireworks,

though we'd been promised war. On television, face after face

was saying, *I am an American.* I wanted to fuck, then shoot

the man who spoke to my mother like a child. I was so afraid

of seeing dead people that I saw them everywhere.

It was the new age. "We" finally had "our own" war.

How can I explain the things and things and things I did wrong?

I was never any good at telling the difference between

what wanted me and what wanted me gone.

I LEARNED THAT I WAS BEAUTIFUL

when J told me what they say

about Asian women. You know what they say.

I didn't, until I did, and it changed everything.

I smiled into the camera, and someone watched.

When I put lipstick on my lips, it made a new word.

I wondered if he would steal me

like he'd stolen my boyfriend's last girlfriend.

Before, I was sweet enough to be let into rooms.

Then I was a red flash among the trees.

Years later, everyone was drunk on confession.

We'd all touched so many people by then;

I was beautiful; I'd grown more feathers. He, blonde,

confessed he'd been watching.

I was beautiful. We found a room with a couch.

My breath flew up into the branches and caught

like a flag. Below, I was unwrapped

and pulling threads of light into my hole.

I wanted the distance between that blonde looking

and my hole to die. I wanted to eat the heavy sun

which had been promised to me.

Here is what is true: he put himself inside

after I said we couldn't. It wasn't the last time

I wanted to slap the light out of me.

Before, I was a strange money. And after.

I stroked his hair

like it was my own hair.

I didn't know until I did:

He put a new word inside me, which rhymed

with the word that was already there.

IN THE AFTERMATH OF THE UNFORGIVABLE, I RAISE MY DOOMED, GREEN HEAD

Atrocity fractals [like a fern].

No more nature metaphors.

It fractals. It itselfs.

: : :

Are you my mother,

ship ablaze on the horizon?

Horizon, are you?

: : :

No war ever ends,

just floats south on the [breeze],

makes new sisters.

: : :

In Laos, it rained yellow.

No word helps me understand

but this: *O, O, O.*

: : :

Someday we'll lie in dirt.

With mouths and mushrooms, the earth

will accept our apology.

UPON LEARNING THAT SOME KOREAN WAR REFUGEES USED PARTIALLY DETONATED NAPALM CANISTERS AS COOKING FUEL

Somewhere in a prior world, a woman with my face

is scraping the seeds from an unborn hell.

All night, doom rang from the sky. And in the morning,

there are mouths to feed. There are crocks in the cellar

and the ruined crops, the early frost, the neighbor's red daughter

strung up in the square. What else to do

when the unspeakable comes. What to burn

when it doesn't. Somewhere in a world that didn't quite

end, a woman like me is foraging for that which failed to kill her.

She is cranking open modernity's throat, wrenching

her arc from its scat. She is a woman who can hack

an impossible morning into water, bean paste, bitter leaves,

another chance to fumble toward the next chance, and the next—

Every day of my life has been something other than my last.

Every day, an extinction misfires, and I put it to work.

UPON LEARNING THAT SOME KOREAN WAR REFUGEES USED PARTIALLY DETONATED NAPALM CANISTERS AS COOKING FUEL

If a partway bomb; if a half-paused hell;

if a killing, failed, can feed;

if a death sentence, incomplete;

if a horror, flopped; if extinction unlocks

its jaw; if what doesn't kill you makes you; if *almost*;

if *never*; if the friction of *did not succeed*; if someone harnessed

annihilation in service of a stew; if someone me-like can see

disaster's refuse and think, *dinner*; if they can gather reeds

and soften them with the genius of unconsummated doom;

if I can almost love the bomb that didn't burst; then,

      if a war didn't end;

if the war that didn't end

helps me eat; if my swelling ends no hunger

but my own; if my hunger ends not a thing;

UPON LEARNING THAT SOME KOREAN WAR REFUGEES USED PARTIALLY DETONATED NAPALM CANISTERS AS COOKING FUEL

How did we get here? you'll think,

kneeling with your neighbors in the parking lot

as the para-police confiscate your coffee.

How did it get to this? everyone will say,

walking north on the interstate as the city's

swarmed in orange, swallowed in smoke.

How did this happen, though it'll be the wrong question,

as they tear open your packages, escort you to a room

where white-knuckled soldiers wait.

Listen: I have a bad imagination.

Dystopia is the word for what's already happened

so many times, it's the reason _____'s so cheap.

No such thing as an undetonated hell;

the pilot light clicks, and I eat.

UPON LEARNING THAT SOME KOREAN WAR REFUGEES USED PARTIALLY DETONATED NAPALM CANISTERS AS COOKING FUEL

I lie on the floor partially bursting, partially stripped by the fact, drowning in the fact, slobbering like a dog in the heat of the fact. Here, on the other side of what happened, I make nothing happen, *nothing, nothing, nothing,* flaccid as a gerund. Dead trees, sharpening the sky. Once upon a time, the people whose nightmares I inherited were safe; then, they weren't. Hence, they were never safe. They survived however they could. They made daughters who married well and were proud in ordinary ways; or they were ashamed. Days passed. They chased vultures from their mothers, were stuffed with bloody rags, watched fire shock their limbs into myth. Days, and days. Here, in the inconceivable future, I am unable. To narrate. To speak in the simple past, facts lined up like soldiers on a horizon. I'm making nothing happen but my own drool, drooling, gaping, chomping at the *ing ing ing.* I make a nothing that whirs into being, feedback looping into a buzz saw of nothing, dome of nothing. So big it rises. Big enough to keep my people safe from the catastrophes that rain from planes. Before each catastrophe, a moment in which my people are safe. Refuge of nothing. Refuge of uneventfulness. First days, then days, and days. In a dead tree's heart, an empty space. In the space, a small animal, useless beautiful animal, stretching its wings, wings, *wings . . .*

UNLOVE POEM

If I call myself unlovable, I am, practically; if I say it
enough times: *unlovable.* Then, like practical magic,

I'm hollow as old garlic; I'm distance-skinned.
I'm a long, mean package, a terror-dyke, a nag, a squinting,

slut-spun hag—it's easy, really. It's the simplest thing,
I do it in my sleep. I have invasive dreams,

after all, they infect my lover's skull, they crank our jaws
into four slow hammers. After all, I'm made of distance

plus the beautiful things people have tried to put
inside me, they fall out the bottom. No one can kill me

with kindness. No one can reach me through the sound
of such ancestral ugly, sound of my grandmothers gagging

a half century ago (did they?). My grandmother beating
her stomach with her fists, drinking medicine, then poison (did she?).

I'm distance-skinned. No one can put a story inside me
but me. If not even my memories love me enough to stay,

then fine, cut off the hands that keep me married
to any history. See? Like magic, then,

I call myself a rotted-out bulb, and soon enough
I'm hauling out the wet stuff, cracking my compost heart

under a shovel's faceless verdict. Sometimes a highway opens
between my hearts, and I run suicides till I'm lactic.

Sometimes I wonder how long I'd have to run
to reach the last generation where one of us felt loved,

and I crumple into carcass. I come from a short line of women
who were handed husbands as salvation from rape.

I'm a short lie of a woman whom men have wanted
to tear apart with their good strong hands. I mean, same.

If I love anyone enough to know they deserve better than me,

and stay anyway, then: What? If I love myself enough to beat

fistfuls of poison into me, into me who hurts me, oh well,

I'm just imitating the rockets' red glare. I'm just covering

the old song. *Unlovable* is open-source, anyone can make up

new verses to sing it. Here's the part where I list the times

my white ex hurt my feelings, or my white teacher,

my white therapist, the white boy who put his dick inside me,

the boy I liked too much, the woman who let me fall

in love with her too fast, of course there's the boy

who died by accident and left me only able to write beautiful poems

about his leaving, pretty only-love things I threw and threw into

the endless distances inside me, highways of quiet.

O, I've been hard to love in America. I've been slow

to speak in America. I've been, undoubtedly, an American
and done practically nothing to stop it. I've been

some version of my grandmothers slinking around the floor
of the GI bar, shivering in the bathroom of the GI bar.

I've been some version of my grandmother making child
after child for a loveless man. I've been her, and I've been

the version of her that lives, that lives in an opportune land,
that chooses who she loves, that sits by a window writing,

drinking water with tulsi, breaking chocolate with her clean hands,
that goes to school after school and collects heart and heart

and heart sweetly brimming in her well-oiled forearms and *still*
has the gall to be unlovable. O, my badly loved grandmothers,

I kin you to me, facelessly. I wrap all our deaths around
my shoulders like a fox pelt coat: grandmother across

oceans and ages, grandmother across the border, grandmother

carried off by soldiers, grandmother carried into endless highway

by disease or dog or dawn's unrelenting purge. I wrap until

I'm made of grandmother, until the ritual musk of their dreams

is sprouting from my skull: sandalwood, ambergris, copper

of blood, coin copper, clay of approaching dusk. I am loved

by pheromone if nothing else. By accident at best.

O beasts of fortune, I am loved sweetest by the horrors of blood,

by my own, and by ours, O blessed root rot, by ours.

III

HOW TO LET GO OF THE WORLD

There's a documentary about climate change called *How to Let Go of the World*, and sam asks, *Should I jump off a building.*

Among a growing list of promises I can't make my friends: *This weight will tether. You can come back up again.* The faithfulness of gravity, of morning sounds. *If only you'll stay.*

⋮

When I walk into the street it's almost as if it'll last: smudge of a cooked orange pressed into the sky. The cars follow all their old lineages back and forth from shifts; meanwhile, three teenagers pile rollicking onto the sidewalk.

I don't know how to do it: hold their faces in my hands and tell them what's waiting. How to teach any of us to follow this song, into what dark.

⋮

One evening, I turned a corner and panicked at a sudden flash in my rearview, teeth chattering into my highest throat. Every nerve prepared for the acrid drip of cop talk until I realized: it was no cruiser. It was the sky. The sky, shocked with dying.

: : :

I cried when I saw the photos of bleached reefs. Later, I had to cut the phrase out of every poem: *Bleached reef. Bleached reef.* If a record skips you bend low to greet it. You greet it with a cloth and your own good breath.

: : :

When the Pyrex burst all over the stove, we stood still for a minute to let ourselves be rocked by the sound, the sudden natural disaster of our ruined dinner. To be safe, we turned to the ceiling and asked any spirits present to tuck themselves back into the drywall. Then went for bags and brooms, picked out the shards, the ghost-knives hiding in the tiles for our heels.

: : :

I should mention that my first love left Earth from a rooftop, though he didn't
jump. Or: he jumped only the way muscles do, on their way to sleep.

: : :

I can watch the videos of brimstone eating California. I can listen to the
sound of a boy describe how holding a line against fire might cut time off his
sentence. I can hold his voice in my hands and whisper straight into it, but
that doesn't make him here. I can love and love his arms helping mine make
something other than dirt and watch that love bleed straight into the space
between us and then of course. It falls. Into a tunnel and gone.

: : :

You can come back up again. Run, and the sky will catch you in its thousand orange

hands. You'll never land.

: : :

I stalk the house swatting the flies, thirsty for the sound of newspaper on

exoskeleton, the satisfaction of a clean and bloody ending.

When they're gone, I almost miss them. *They fly out of my arms. I fly out of their*

arms.

: : :

What's the German word for preemptively missing something so much you

can't look at it. Literal translation: *green green green and I hide my face.*

: : :

In Flint I turn on the tap and out comes war wrapped in putrid cellophane. In Detroit I flip the switch and boil war for tea. In Providence I over-war the plants. War runs down my face in the theater's dark. I wade into a blanket of war and let its waves carry me out, out past the shoreline's certainty.

: : :

In other words: I beach myself.

Other words: I leech bleakly. Breathe sleet, a wreath of it. I flinch at the leaves, anticipating their reek, the graves of reefs. I bleach and bleach and watch the chlorine slip clean from my teeth.

: : :

I want to tether my friends to the rooftop railing the way we once pinned a blanket to the beach with shoes, books, bags of carrots, wine in a can. How we flexed and curled our toes until we found the damper sand, the soft homes of crabs below. But the wind won't stop coming. Orange and exoskeleton against our little shore.

: : :

If only it'd been a ghost that had shattered the glass. Some simple anger— some old fable we could soothe back to sleep with a few choice words and a handful of incense. Much worse that it was the heat. Much worse: the way molecules bend to the fact of it, and break.

: : :

I listened to those firefighters while, in Hamtramck, I waged a much tinier war against the dust on my blinds. I wiped and wiped to rid my windows of it. In the forest, rot feeds. The earth drinks soot and makes it into new leaves. In other words it's the plastic, here, that makes dirt a problem.

I bent low to greet it, dipped a cloth in water to approximate a tongue. Meanwhile, the light through the slats shocked my image into slices.

: : :

When disaster comes, some of us will stand on the rooftop to address the ghosts. Some of us will hold the line. Some will look for the shards, run our tongues along the floor.

: : :

I say *when* like disaster hasn't come, isn't already growing in the yard. Do I have to run through the list? The firefighter prisoners—my friends' islands slowly swallowed—war in my faucet, remember? *Syrian Civil War* is the name of a drought. The name of this hurricane is Exxon, *Exxon*, I shout. I can pull as many weeds as I want. I stalk the garden pulling them, thirsty for the sound of their true names wrenching out of the soil. (Do I have to say it? They fly out of my arms.)

: : :

I should mention that when my first love died, I already had a stack of poems about missing him. I want to say this prepped me for widowhood— widowhood to the world, et cetera.

The truth: under the topmost sand is another, darker layer, damp from the ocean's closeness. There were days I begged to be buried in it—cool, mutable grave, reprieve from the unrelenting sun—sun—sun—

: : :

Among a growing list of other things that are unrelenting: teenagers piling rollicking into the street. The shock of a citrus sky in midwinter. The way a phrase's shape can hook itself through your lip for weeks. Once, sam walked around a whole day muttering, *Soul, I say!* and he did, and did.

: : :

In lieu of a proper translation for my grief, I say, *green green green*, until it cools enough to lower myself into.

: : :

Holding my love's face in my hands, I tell him I miss him. I say, *I miss you like I miss the trees.*

By this I mean, *Look! The trees are here! Everyone's outside, darling: green in my hands, ghosts in the drywall—everyone's waiting for us.*

: : :

I should mention that when my first love died, he was already dead, had already always been on his way to the roof, on his way over its edge. And when he was here, he was here. By this logic, he is and was and is and was. Unrelentingly.

: : :

In lieu of proximity to firefighters; in lieu of the ability to speak the airless language of ghosts; or to reverse the logic of molecules; or to force Exxon to call the hurricane by its rightful name; or to convince my friends not to launch themselves from the rooftops of every false promise made by every rotten idol; in lieu of all I can't do or undo; I hold. The faces of the trees in my hands. I miss them. And miss and miss them. Until I fly out of grief's arms, and the sky. Catches me in its thousand orange hands. It catches me, and I stay there. Suspended against the unrelenting orange. I stay there splayed, and dying. And shocking the siren sky.

IV

Then I'd sing, 'cause I'd know
I'd know how it feels
I'd know how it feels to be free.

—*Nina Simone*

AARON SAYS THE WORLD IS UPSIDE DOWN

and it's true, the cops are shooting rubber bullets at even the blonde

journalists now; the Target is on fire, and the Wells Fargo's shining

face kicked in by white boys with gas masks and hammers trying

to jump-start their war—and yet, the upside-down world is also,

by definition, the same world, like the map that hung in the hallway

of the house where I lived three or four lives ago, Argentina at the top,

Greenland kissing its toes; it was a metaphor, someone explained,

for seeing things another way—so yes, if it is true that another killer

cop's killed another Black child's father, another "unauthorized" choke-

hold, another no charge again, if once more riot gear again budget once

again gas station, more flames, more who's to blame gets blamed again

if again and again it is the same—then it holds that the opposite must also

be true: the so-called opposite world of food drop-off stations,

of phone trees, of bailouts and carry an extra mask, the world of kneeling

for a stranger's gift of milk to flush the tear gas, the world

of saying a thing in unison so clear it drills a hole through to the other

side of what's possible, so clear and wholly inverted, we realize it's been here

all along: O kingdom of fire, O kingdom of food, with the same mouth

we take your blessings; with the same mouth we pronounce you come.

FIELD TRIP TO THE MUSEUM OF HUMAN HISTORY

Everyone had been talking about the new exhibit,

recently unearthed artifacts from a time

no living hands remember. What twelve-year-old

doesn't love a good scary story? Doesn't thrill

at rumors of her own darkness whispering

from the canyon? We shuffled in the dim light

and gaped at the secrets buried

in clay, reborn as warning signs:

a "nightstick," so called for its use

in extinguishing the lights in one's eyes.

A machine used for scanning fingerprints

like cattle ears, grain shipments. We shuddered,

shoved our fingers in our pockets, acted tough.

Pretended not to listen as the guide said,

Ancient American society was built on competition

and maintained through domination and control.

In place of our modern-day accountability practices,

the institution known as "police" kept order

using intimidation, punishment, and force.

We pressed our noses to the glass,

strained to imagine strangers running into our homes,

pointing guns in our faces because we'd hoarded

too much of the wrong kind of "property."

Jadera asked something about redistribution

and the guide spoke of safes, evidence rooms,

more profit. Marian asked about raiding the rich,

and the guide said, *In America, there were no greater*

protections from police than wealth and whiteness.

Finally, Zaki asked what we were all wondering:
But what if you didn't want to?

and the walls snickered and said, *steel,*
padlock, strip search, hard stop.

Dry-mouthed, we came upon a contraption
of chain and bolt, an ancient torture instrument

the guide called "hand-cuffs." We stared
at the diagrams and almost felt

the cold metal licking our wrists, almost tasted dirt,
almost heard the siren and slammed door,

the cold-blooded click of the cocked-back pistol,
and our palms were slick with some old recognition,

as if in some forgotten dream we had lived this way,

in submission, in fear, assuming positions

of power were earned, or at least carved in steel,

that they couldn't be torn down like musty curtains,

an old house cleared of its dust and obsolete artifacts.

    We threw open the doors to the museum,

shedding its nightmares on the marble steps,

and bounded into the sun, toward the school buses

or toward home, or the forests, or the fields,

or wherever our good legs could roam.

ON HOW

after Nate

we wrote new chants

& bailed folks out

& plate-scooped meals

& healed old wounds

& walked cold blocks

& drummed up, stumped

& "stole" back land

& claimed back facts

& sewed loud flags

& sowed right crops

& cut cops' cash

& heaved gold rot

& let go ghosts

& surged, rode crests

& spread wealth flat

& clawed down walls

& ex-learned harm

& nixed cruel laws

& crowdsourced grace

& ground teeth down

& laid cards flat

& dug toward hope

& sang off-key

& worked through shit

& took sweet time

& pre-lived worlds

& dreamed past doom

& walked, fell, walked,

fell, walked, fell, walked.

TOWARD GRACE

In this version, that girl the reporters dubbed "Grace"

scribbles homework. Is time-rich, abundant with grace.

Out the window, world sings in the key of magnolia,

and magnolia drips gifts of right answers for Grace.

For some brains, time bends, like the sheet-face of lakes.

Call it *deficit*. Some pinball, constellate our own grace.

Online, blondes chirp tips, spin fidgets, get follows.

Old story: unequal distribution of grace.

Imagine a version where Black children, too,

can be children, make mistakes, still anticipate grace.

My mother, unmothered, grew death-quick. She raised

her three siblings herself. Later, chose her name: Grace.

She's a healer now, Mother. And healing. Mends bones,
orders meds, prays, remembers. Is making her grace.

Land that won't love us back, of thee, of thee.
To be loved without reason is the dreamsong of grace.

This version: no school stripped by crisis and market
steals time, care, or tutors law-promised to Grace.

This version: *school*'s the name for any garden or place
that loves Black and brown kids toward their brilliance, grace.

In this version: no Zoom judge, no prison for children.
No prison for children. No Zoom sentence for Grace.

Every day, she is healing. Mends hurts, scribbles answers.
Magnolia. Imagine: magnolia for Grace.

I reach toward the sound of this anthem, this whistle.

This poem is a reach-machine, outstretched toward Grace.

My lake-brain; my time-slide; unequal song, yes, of brain.

Still, I'll version it: care-time for you, us, kin, Grace.

PRAYER FOR THE UNTRANSLATED TESTIMONY

Midnight, and I'm sitting on the back steps

looking at the leaves and listening to the sound

a boy is making into the night with the peak

of his lungs, somewhere in my neighborhood.

He is stretching the air, and I do not

know what it means, this sound.

It sounds, I think, like a name, like the name

of my friend Fatimah, *Fatimah*, but with different

letters, I think, or maybe it sounds like a command,

a long and desperate spell, which he makes of the air again

and again and now growing longer as he shouts it;

and if I ask my heart, rude translator though it is,

to read back this sound, what I hear rippling

from the quiet floor of my chest is *let me in*

let me in, or *open it, open it*, and now in my chest's

vocabulary there is also a door. There is also a blue

light in the top window and a face that will not

appear. And some of my friends, I know, have names

that sound like this, like *I am here, I am here*, like

why won't you answer, like *why can't you see me* and they are, mostly, not boys, but do grow long and blue-lit

at midnight. They are spells, the women I know,

and today, a woman sat in front of a panel

of men who, I have to try to believe, were too

once boys who shivered in the yard, a woman sat

and had to say again and again, *it happened,*

it happened, and watch the glass panes of the once-

boys' faces remain unlit and only echoing back,

with their short vocabularies, *are you sure, are you sure,*

are you sure. So tonight, reaching up to hold hands

with these leaves stretching onto the back steps,

I say: Please. Let this spell grow legs. Let my sisters' names

grow long as their hair. Long as they need to.

Let their names rattle the night air with their

incessant lungs. Let the sounds of their names burn

blue in the night, let even their ugliest memories

be named after the daughters of prophets, please,

if there is a god named for the humble undersides

of these leaves somehow not yet dead, let

the names of my sisters make all the doors on my street

fly open. Let every tree sleeping in our chests

claw awake. And rush out to answer that call.

COALITIONAL CENTO

you wake up and you unremember the world

what an honor to inhabit   the cleanest air

what a superpower to be

great-grandmother chanting mantras

      in a circle of salt

I dream of things that are larger than life

I can walk the streets at any time of the day

      am I the colonization or the reparations?

I, too, make the decision. I carry it with me

connect the dots in our real lives

ginger roots cross mountains

we will not live quietly

I choose to be the reparations

WITH MOUTHS AND MUSHROOMS, THE EARTH WILL ACCEPT OUR APOLOGY

When Hiroshima was destroyed by an atomic bomb in 1945, it is said, the
first living thing to emerge from the blasted landscape was a matsutake
mushroom.

—Anna Lowenhaupt Tsing, *The Mushroom at the End of the World*

made of shock doctrine, made of root-chatter,

made of playgrounds blackened with corpses,

made of the anti-modern, of hell-wreck, made of symbiotic

destruction, of parasite and pericapitalism, made of slave trade,

of wretched, made of reek and reason, made of ex-flesh, of cells

stampeding through the lungs of miners, made of morals, of mortals,

of *everything went with perfection*, made of infants in horse stalls

or strapped in reddened rags, made of sour rice, of phlegm,

of warp and spore, made of forest floor dis-

enfranchised to dust, of sun-laden and empty space, made

of empty space, made of timber price, of sugarcane,

of nematode and elite sleaze, of seamstresses diving to concrete,

made of trash-bellied caribou, of suicide pact, of hands deep

in the throat of a comfort girl, made of entrails, of gromet, of every chipper *we can do it*, made of sacred land, of funeral scream,

of holy water and flayed graves, made of stolen names, of commerce,

of conquistador, of near-death visions on the factory floor, made of

the unforgivable future, and the unforgivable past, i bloom,

bloodless, and ready to feed.

WILDLIFE

In the Canadian province of Alberta, a massive wildlife—uh, wildfire—
exploded to ten times its previous size Thursday.

—Amy Goodman, *Democracy Now!*, 2016

They say the blast was triggered by a passenger pigeon's ghostly

coo, swifting over the oil fields—at which the grasses stiffened,

shot up a warning scent—which made the beetles shudder from

their beds—which spread a rumor among the earthworms, until,

so quietly at first that no one noticed, a thin hoof cracked

open a patch of earth: last spring's last-born caribou, the one

who'd gotten separated from the herd and gutted by flies, now back

and raising an orchestra of dust with its kicking, calling forth

hoof by hoof, the whole herd, stampeding from their graves,

flesh and fur remapping onto bones as they percussed out,

pulling with them the pine martens and black-footed ferrets,

who regathered their bones from the soil and darted up

to hop aboard the pine trees now rushing from the horizon,

stretching their newborn necks toward the sun's familiar laugh

as shrikes and warblers flocked giddy to their shoulders, *we're back,*

we're back, they giggled as firs and ferns yawned upright to marry

the sparrows and the softshell turtles, whose humble jaws birthed

ponds and marshes with each exhale, inviting the whooping cranes

to unfurl their bodies from the wind and gladly, gladly swoop

down to bless the fish, which in turn gave the whales the idea

to distill back into their old forms from the clouds overhead, until

the sky was clogged with blubbery gods—right whales, gray, beluga,

and even a rumor of a blue whale somewhere over Calgary, casting

a great gray shadow over the baseball fields, every parking lot

and highway cracking open as the earth remembered, rejoiced

with its remembering—and as some of the humans kept trying

to drag up the earth's black blood, to sell off their mothers'

old marrow, suddenly, then, each pump and spigot spouted forth bees,

butterflies, short-horned lizards, plovers and prickly pears, grizzlies,

snakes, owls of all feather and shape, shrews, sturgeon, each drop

of oil renouncing its war draft and returning to its oldest names:

muscle; stamen; tooth; shell; the land and water laughing aloud,

a laugh that spread the way a fever spreads, like the opposite of death—

just the earth, with its thousand mouths, singing: *I will. I will.*

THINGS THAT ALREADY GO PAST BORDERS

trade deals; pathogens; specific

passports; particular skill sets; vegetables; car

parts; streaming rights; seasonal workers; some

insects; certain birds; religion; dialect; music

at the right volume; headlights; human

remains; wireless signals; all manner

of money; of memory; people

in trucks; on trains; on foot; in line, in

lines; charging checkpoints; wading waist deep

through rivers; clinging to rafts; or yawning

their way through customs; sisters

separated for decades, whose faces

are as foreign to each other as the faces of

the dead; seeds; drones; prisoners

on planes; dictators in motorcades; orders

to kill; and longing; yes, this

most of all; the longing

of families; and the long

-ing of storms

DEMILITARIZED ZONE

I roll my suitcase through the demilitarized airport. I hand my demilitarized ticket to the demilitarized agent at the gate, who smiles in a demilitarized way, points with an open hand. On the plane, I order a demilitarized orange juice. I look down at the demilitarized mountains of Siberia and imagine walking on them. We land on the demilitarized runway, and the captain's voice over the loudspeaker is demilitarized as he asks us to stay in our seats. In the bathroom, I brush my demilitarized teeth. I get on the wrong demilitarized train and have to plead with the conductor who does not have a gun. I watch the demilitarized pine trees filter the sun like a ceiling fan. I watch demilitarized cranes land on a lake so bright it makes me blink. The demilitarized conductor bows as he enters each train car; an old woman sits with demilitarized bundles wrapped in pink. At Pyeongyang I stop for demilitarized noodles. The Taedong River is not full of bodies. The sun in the trees makes a noise like *eeeeee! eeeeee!* The sparrows in the buckwheat fields shout in northern accents and no guns. At Ŭiju the platform is demilitarized; the taxi stand is not pockmarked with mines; I buy a demilitarized barley tea, and the shopkeeper hands me my change like she's responsible for me. In the demilitarized record hall, I hand over a slip of demilitarized paper, and the clerk smiles at my accent. *You've traveled a long way*, she says as she leads me to the demilitarized stacks. We find my family's genealogy book. We turn to the last generation recorded before the world ended and our line split south. I unfold my paper with the list of missing names. The clerk copies the letters as I read them. Together, we demilitarize my family. The sun coming in through the windows says, *ah. ah.*

DISPATCHES FROM A FUTURE GREAT-GREAT-GRANDDAUGHTER

Dear Improbable You,

What was it like to live so gridded? So trackchanges?

So carceral, somnambulant, asphyxiating at split screens

while Nation glowered with rot? What was it like

to slouch numb-faced here and watch your image

get dirty with Algorithm elsewhere, shuffle into destiny's schlep?

Did your pulse come haptic? Did you pay money for food?

Did you dial three numbers and salute genocidaires

with crestwhitened incisors when they knocked? Did you pray

ever? Hope, any? Or did you take a number,

snatch what scraps you could, and pet your children?

Everything was happening, and you were alive.

You were alive then. What did you do?

    : : :

Great-Great-Grandmother, I'm writing to you

under chartreuse skies, after the Great Verticality,

and after the Multiwars and their Various Rebrandings,

and after Tipping Points #1–379,

and after, finally, the Very Long, Very Slow Dispersal of Things.

I wonder if you can imagine it: the tall tall oceans,

the smell of sick-gas (weirdly sweet) and sani-spray

(like if toothpaste were a vegetable), the rhythm of jumpdancers

on the boardwalks, water swinging in barrels, grass-fed grass.

There are twelve different siren patterns, one for each kind of crisis:

two honks for fire; three short trills for a runaway brain;

a Loneliness Emergency is a low swoop followed by a chirp;

and so on. There are crises every day, and there's also bread

bubbling on the counter, pickled beans, a cat who comes home.

What I want you to know is that we're okay. Hurting

but okay. We're surviving, though it's true,

we don't know what that means, exactly.

: : :

Some rituals I do to imagine what you knew about freedom:

    move my fingers over glass, swipe like a question;

    swallow a bullet and stay silent until it passes;

    touch my lips to silicone, sand, silicone, sand;

    walk into the ocean and let the waves kick me over,

        then dry in the sun and lick the salt from my forearms;

sit facing a friend and hold our palms together without touching;

    take turns completing the phrase, *It could have been that* . . . ;

draw my face from memory;
ask a friend to bind me with rope until I can't move, tense up until I cry;

    then laugh until the ties loosen; until everything loosens;

    : : :

Dear Great-Great-Grandsomeone,

Under a graphless sky, I'm writing to say: thank you for healing
what you could; for passing down what you couldn't.

I'm plentituding what I can; what I can't, I let tunnel me
like roughage, like a "bullet," like a slur I won't daycare.

What you gave me isn't wisdom, and I have no wisdom in return,
just handfuls of lifestock: Every day, a sky is.

Miles are. We sing, entangled, and the root-world answers,
and together we're making. Something of it. Something

of all those questions you left.

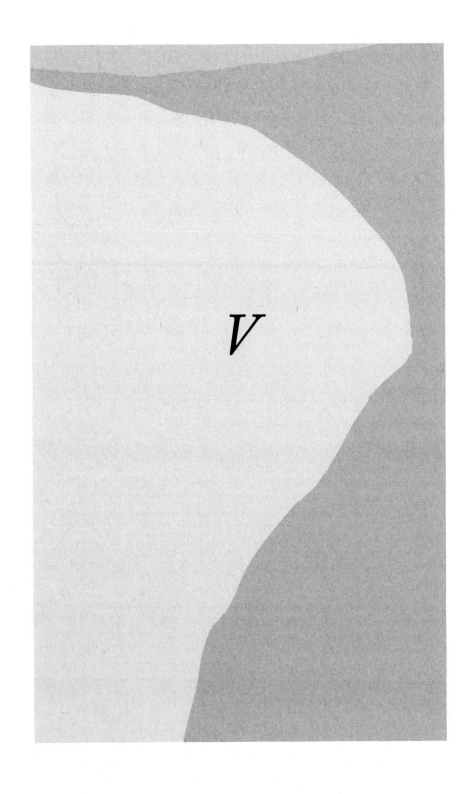

V

LOOK

My mother, very Catholic, loves that song: *Imagine*
there's no heaven. Can you picture it?—my mother
joining the chorus of her three churchless children to croon,
no heaven, no hell, nothing before or after? Above us,
only the universe and its borderless yawn. Only the trees
who died for my handwriting, history's pollen, fields
and field hands I can't stop robbing with money.
Today, I woke up on still-stolen land, then scrolled
through the latest debris of people attempting godliness
in a hundred wrong ways. The room was filled today
with light; filled, you could say, with nothing. No hope,
no glory. No such peach as an ethical peach.
The minute I started wanting paradise, it leapt
from my belief. I'm not good enough to survive
not being good. I'm like you—still drooling
after a perfect world, even as the stars warble
off-key and the oceans rattle with plastics.
Imagine, I can't stop saying. *Imagine*, I beg,
when I should have said, *Look*: paradise
is both a particle and a wave. You don't have
to believe in something for it to startle you awake.

DOOM

You've dreamt about it since you were a kid:

a secret, a funeral, a spreading cough, and then

it starts—the end. The whole, terrible end.

For years, you've kept one eye on the shadows

swilling above the door, waiting for the arrival

of the God of Doom. What to do now

that he's here, sipping coffee in our kitchen?

We sneak glares from the sink, mutter apologies

when we bump in the hall. He's an awful guest,

of course—tracks blood everywhere, cries

when we feed him, screams if we don't.

So we keep the freezer stocked with dumplings, black fruit,

beans to last a month. We take turns hefting his bulk,

keep him placated with a soundtrack of pickaxes, songs

about death camps and microplastics, circular fretting,

it's only a matter of time. When it storms, he yanks open

the windows; he polishes our worst parts; steals, constantly.

At night, he raps at the wall behind our heads, just

as he did for ten thousand nights before he showed up,

just as he'll do for ten thousand nights after.

Meanwhile—well, you know. Meanwhile.

All our kin is dying at a distance.

The coast's been burning for weeks. Filling the kettle,

you catch me humming, *The dream that you dream*

will come true, and we laugh, though nothing's funny

but this: We knew the end was coming here. We knew it,

and like idiots—like perfect idiots—we stayed.

WASTE

I look at your face and there, I feel it—my life

rushing toward me from both directions, twin rivers reversed

and crashing backwards into their source. You were improbable as that—

your eyes flicking open a seam in the dark, improbable—

us, laughing at the same time with both our heads on the same

pink pillow, improbable—in the same city—both our hearts

still going—*What are the chances*, I murmur when I reach out

and touch your brow, *How is this possible—*

: : :

You only knew him for two years! cries the mother

of the boy we lost—sweet bedraggled flourish of a boy

who was hers and hers and hers and briefly mine and then—

out—like a swath of river, over a cliff and gone,

over (be specific) the side of a building and gone, back into

whatever name the universe calls us away toward, leaving question

after question in his unending wake, his wake shrinking

into a red horizon. Two years we fell into somehow step.

Where is your son? asks the chatty lady at the counter, and it's not

a bad question, just an impossible one—*where*   *is*

                               your   *son where*

                    is   *your son*

    : : :

I'm here, on the pillow, watching your eyes move all

on their own, tracing a thought as it crawls across the ceiling.

I'm here—trying to memorize the details, reciting them like a song—

little crust in his eye / bit of bristle on his chin / o smell of him / him / him—

Once, in a fit of panic, I lie upside down and study your ankles,

interrogate each scar, marry the lot with my mortal mouth, hurry—

before we're all washed out into that infinite downstream.

I imagine decades with your head between my palms and feel

only terror at the loss—I'm here—*O him—I have wasted my life—*

    : : :

I admit, there was a someone who came into my life

like an oak floor under my grief-thin air. For six years he held my world

in his hands. What happened between us is a silence, and silence is all

that happened after. Let's just say I walked away as if I deserved

my own years. Let's say it, and be clear—I deserve nothing.

I deserve to be deserted in the woods, chasing the smell of smoke,

if *smoke* is what I call the nights I begged like an animal, the thickness

of a heart, the slime of it, green-eyed daughters whose ghosts

I tore to shreds, then pinned on him. I can't say anything yet

but this: It was me who brought the cliff, pushed us off.

It was me who ended that world.

: : :

Scrambled by need, I say, *I want to give you my bones*, all

my language rendered useless at your feet. I'm useless, here, too—I thrust

my uselessness at you. I say and say it: I want to be scraped across the bed like

a salt-slick meal. I want to be torn from my frame, steamed clean. *I want to be*

nothing, said the man in the story before he nearly got his wish, wrecked and reddened in the alley—and it's like catching my face in a car window,

dusk-addled negative mouthing along to my neediest self. *I want to be nothing,*

as you push your knuckles into my mouth. *I want* to be nothing, a wordless

evening opening around you. I want no memory before or after,

just this—my hips lifting off the mattress, cracked and spilling, wingless,

my certain brain spread across time's horror-lines, so I can lift each memory

from its sour bath, hold it up to the lamp in your mouth.

. : :

Yes, I squandered years in houses promised to ruin.

There were particular futures I could not bear, though they rushed

toward my keening, fogbell mouth. For years, I was hot with that siren,

sweaty with doomsday's moans. I lathered my skin in hopelessness.

O, it was better that way—to be streaked with the prophecy

of a dark field, bordered on one end by love-as-imprisonment,

as husbandry, a price to being touched, a historical and

therefore unsurprising cage writhing with tongues. On the other end: grief

and its endlessly fabulous outfits; feathers for weeks; tulle.

And in the swath between them, loneliness. Just that: loneliness.

I thought that was all love could give me. I'm sorry. I thought I'd seen

the future. I thought I knew the words to our one wild

and unfathomable life. Forgive me; I see it now. I wasted

so much time being wrong.

PROTEST POEM

The air's so thick

with fury it shakes

the windows. Nothing

cuts through walls

like rage

and its promises: *No peace*

is a drill—joy

you have to charge

to make work; the cheer

that follows each

verse, an ekphrastic

for the as-yet-

unbuilt museum

of what we had to survive

to make paradise

from its ruins.

                It's okay

if you don't believe me.

No one could have told me

I was possible

with a sentence

that would have made it

true. So: this isn't

a sentence.

It's a sound.

It's a blade,

spinning. It's a wave

that stutters

at the air until

the plate glass

cracks.

NOTES

"The World Keeps Ending and the World Goes On" borrows a line from Martín Espada's "Imagine the Angels of Bread."

"Catastrophe Is Next to Godliness" was written after a scene in Ling Ma's *Severance*.

"Poem with an End in Sight" borrows a line from Suji Kwock Kim's "The Chasm."

"Science Fiction Poetry" and "I Learned That I Was Beautiful" borrow lines from Lucille Clifton. Thank you, too, Lucille, for the first poem in the "Upon Learning" series.

"Comfort Poem" borrows lines from Langston Hughes and Emily Dickinson.

"Upon Learning That Some Korean War Refugees Used Partially Detonated Napalm Canisters as Cooking Fuel" makes reference to works by Grace M. Cho and Suji Kwock Kim.

"How to Let Go of the World" borrows language from sam sax, Laura Brown-Lavoie, Bhanu Kapil, and Martín Espada.

"Field Trip to the Museum of Human History" was written after a scene in Ursula K. Le Guin's *The Dispossessed*, and owes its life to my movement family in Providence, Rhode Island.

"On How" owes its heartbeat to the poem "fiddy'leven" by Nate Marshall.

"Toward Grace" is for the Michigan student (referred to in news media by her middle name, Grace) who was incarcerated in a juvenile detention facility during the COVID-19 pandemic for falling behind on her remote schoolwork, despite having been denied certain accommodations under her individualized education plan for ADHD.

"Coalitional Cento" is made up of lines by Othelia Jumapao, Sonam Wangmo, Afifa Shoket Kohli, Natasha Akery, lee ol therese, Geena Chen, Bianca Soonja Kim, and Jordan Furtak, written in response to prompts I posted online during Asian Pacific American History Month 2021. Thank you all for writing and imagining with me.

"With Mouths and Mushrooms" includes a quote by US Navy captain William Sterling Parsons, who served as mission commander on the *Enola Gay*'s bombing of Hiroshima. The poem owes its life to Anna Lowenhaupt Tsing's *The Mushroom at the End of the World*, Peter Blow's documentary *Village of Widows* (1999), and David Eng's work on the Sahtu Dene people's reparations work in relation to Japanese and Korean hibakusha.

"Waste" includes a line from Garth Greenwell's "Gospodar," and a nod, of course, to Mary Oliver.

Additionally, many of these poems owe their lives to the work and voices of Ross Gay, Aracelis Girmay, Brenda Shaughnessey, Ilya Kaminsky, Patricia Smith, Jamaal May, Justin Phillip Reed, Sumita Chakraborty, Carl Phillips, Evie Shockley, Tim Donnelly, Grace M. Cho, Emily Jungmin Yoon, Alexis Pauline Gumbs, adrienne maree brown, Don Mee Choi, Daniel Borzutsky, Douglas Kearney, Cathy Park Hong, Rita Dove, Linda Gregerson, Tung-Hui

Hu, Eve L. Ewing, Angel Nafis, sam sax, Cameron Awkward-Rich, everyone in Dark Noise, probably every poet I'm lucky enough to call a friend, and many others whose words and wisdom have soaked into my brain, whether I'm smart enough to realize it or not.

ACKNOWLEDGMENTS

Grateful acknowledgment is made to the editors of the following journals, in which poems first appeared, sometimes in earlier versions or with different titles:

Poetry: "The World Keeps Ending, and the World Goes On" and "We Used Our Words We Used What Words We Had"

The Atlantic: "Catastrophe Is Next to Godliness," "Danez Says They Want to Lose Themselves in Bops They Can't Sing Along To," "Disaster Means 'Without a Star,'" and "Look"

The New Republic: "Good Morning America"

Paris Review: "Amid Rising Tensions on the Korean Peninsula"

Indiana Review: "September 2001"

American Poetry Review: "Unlove Poem" and the "Upon Learning That Some Korean Refugees . . ." series

PEN Poetry Series: "How to Let Go of the World"

PBS NewsHour: "Field Trip to the Museum of Human History"

Lantern Review: "Prayer for the Untranslated Testimony" and "Demilitarized Zone"

Under a Warm Green Linden: "Wildlife"

Thank you to my brilliant, generous editor, the incomparable Jenny Xu. Thank you to Annie Hwang, Leslie Shipman, and everyone at Ecco, APL, and the Shipman Agency for all of your work ferrying this project—and my life around it—into possibility. Thank you to the Gaius Charles Bolin Fellowship and the Serenbe Artist in Residence Program, which provided time and space to write this book, and to Hieu Minh Nguyen, for organizing the retreat where the first version of this manuscript materialized. I'm forever grateful to be in community with Jamila, Fati, Danez, Aaron, Nate, Paula, sam, Hieu, Safia, Alison, Kaveh, Laura, Hanif, Angel, Shira, Eve, Daniel, Ydalmi, Itzel, Jina, Britt, Ren-yo, Elliott, Andrea, VyVy, Ceci, Crystal, Amina, Sarah, Phil, Bao, Terisa, No'u, Cynthia, Jess, Vivian, Bernie, MARS, Tamiko, Lo, Nathan, Justice, Brittany, Ajanaé, and the many, many others who have made it possible for me to have a brain, a heart, a writing life. Thank you to the many teachers whose voices were in the room each time I sat down to this book. I'm grateful always for the love, lessons, and fortitude of my family: Umma, Appa, Brigid, Paul, DC, Jenny. To my dear Cameron: you make *here* good and *elsewhere* possible; I would be lost, in so many ways, without you. And finally, to the teachers, organizers, artists, scholars, facilitators, healers, land defenders, and movement workers who are building the worlds to come: thank you, thank you, thank you.